MAKING ART WITH SAND AND EARTH

Gillian Chapman & Pam Robson

PowerKiDS press.

New York

All projects should be done carefully, with an adult's help and supervision whe **appropriate (especially for activities involving any cutting, carving, or sewing). A** **adult should execute or supervise any work with a craft knife, and safety scissor** **should be used for all cutting.**

Published in 2008 by The Rosen Publishing Group, Inc.
29 East 21st Street, New York, NY 10010

Copyright © 2008 Wayland/The Rosen Publsihing Group, Inc.

First Edition

Picture Acknowledgments
Life File 4 (Emma Lee), 5t (Nicola Sutton),
5b (Sue Davies)

Library of Congress Cataloging-in-Publication Data

Chapman, Gillian.
    Making art with sand and earth / Gillian Chapman & Pam Robson.
    -- 1st ed. p. cm. -- (Everyday art)
    Includes index.
    ISBN-13: 978-1-4042-3723-0 (library binding)
    ISBN-10: 1-4042-3723-2 (library binding)
    1.Plaster craft--Juvenile literature. 2.Sand casting--Juvenile literature.
    3.Nature craft--Juvenile literature. 4.Straw work--Juvenile literature.
    5.Recycling (Waste, etc.)--Juvenile literature. I. Robson, Pam. II. Title
TT160.C4923 2007
745.5--dc22

                                    2006030137

Manufactured in China

Contents

Resources from Earth

Earth's Resources

People have always used the Earth's natural resources to make things to meet their needs. Long ago, easily found resources were used to make basic necessities, such as food, shelter, and clothing. Today, technology makes it possible to get resources in hard-to-reach places. These resources can be used to manufacture (or make) things. In making these materials, large amounts of energy are consumed, and cannot be replaced. Renewable energy can be replaced. Using natural, renewable materials avoids this energy waste.

Traditional Pottery Vase from Morocco in North Africa

History and Technology

Technology moves forward when people discover new ways of using materials. The earliest civilizations learned that clay could be molded to make pots. The first bricks were shaped thousands of years ago, when clay combined with straw was discovered to be a good building material. By 2500 B.C., the Bronze Age had begun.

People had realized that copper and tin could be combined to make bronze. The Iron Age began with the smelting of iron from iron-bearing rocks (getting metal from its ore). Alloys like steel appeared in the nineteenth century. The twentieth century may perhaps be remembered as the Plastic Age—plastic is a material that creates big recycling problems.

Out of the Earth

Most people feel the need to have beautiful things around them. The earliest examples of arts and crafts were created from Earth's rocks, minerals, and soils. Sculptures were carved, clay was molded. The first artists took all their raw materials from the Earth —dyes, sands, and clays. Artists' tools were made by shaping available natural objects like flint. Cave paintings can still be seen today. A belief in powerful spirits of the natural world inspired this traditional art. Wall paintings of traditional homes in Northern Ghana are created with paints made from earth pigments. Traditionally, the Navajo Indians have relied upon the magic of their sand paintings to dispel evil and cure ills.

In Zimbabwe, Africa, village women weave baskets from natural fibers.

Aboriginal rock paintings at Ubirri Rock, Kakadu, Australia.

On the Earth

The Earth also supports an ecosystem of animals and plants. Many of these plants and animals provided the first raw materials used by artists. Fibers, fleece, and hair were spun, dyed, and woven. Found objects gave artists ideas. Wood was carved and chiseled, and bark provided a good surface to paint on. Aboriginal Dreamtime art was—and is— created with sticks and natural pigments.

Saving the Earth

When you use renewable materials in arts and crafts projects, you are doing your part to help save Earth's resources.

Sand Painting

Seashore Sands

Seashore sands are found in a range of shades, from black to white. Old lava flows make black sands; shells and skeletons of marine life make white sands. On Tahiti, beaches protected from the wind are bright white, but those facing into the wind are black. Seashore materials have many different textures, from fine-grained sands to huge cobble stones.

Desert sands

Desert sands can also have different colors and textures depending on the type of rock from which they are formed. Quartz is the most common mineral found in sand. It comes from granite, a rock found worldwide.

Navajo Sand Art

The Navajo believe that sand paintings can have great powers. For example, a sand painting might be created to cure a sick child. The child sits in the middle while the colored sands, mixed with charcoal and other materials, trickle through the fingers of the healer, forming a painting on the ground. After the ritual, the painting is erased.

Colored Sand Jars

It is very simple to color sand. Use clean, fine sand. First, sift it to remove any large pieces of grit and shell. Carefully mix the sand with powder paint to make a range of different colored sands. Spoon layers of sand into clear glass jars. Practice making patterns in the sand by pushing a piece of wire or a flexible plastic stick between the sand and the glass. If you put a layer of soil on top of the sand, then you can grow small cactus plants in the sand jars.

Colored Sand Jars

Colored Sands

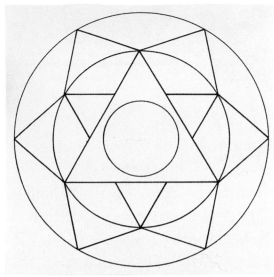

Mandala Design

Sand Mandalas

Mandala is the Sanskrit for "circle" Mandalas are created by Tibetan monks, and colored sands are used for special occasions. Usually, the sands are made from precious stones. The Buddhist mandala is thought to have special power and energy.

The circular pattern is first drawn in white ink. Then, beginning in the middle, streams of colored sands are poured through metal funnels. The mandalas are also temporary works of art. After their ceremonial use, they are taken apart.

Making a Sand Mandala

Sketch a circular pattern on cardboard. Carefully paste craft glue over the areas of the design that will be covered with the same colored sand. Make a paper funnel and slowly trickle colored sand onto the glue. Allow the glue to dry and brush away any extra sand before continuing. Use one color at a time, filling in the pattern, until the sand mandala is complete.

Coloring the Mandala with the Sand

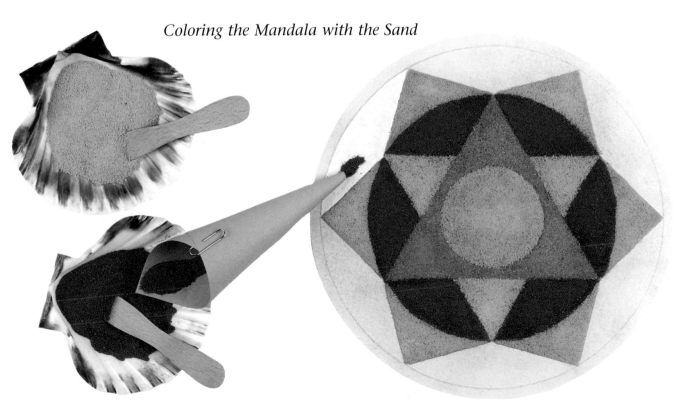

Sand Molds

Grains of Sand

Sand forms from worn-away pieces of rock. It is made up of different minerals and grains of quartz, and is sometimes described as powdered silica. The grains are between 0.002 in (0.06 mm) and 0.08 in (2 mm) across. Grains of silt, or mud, are smaller than this; larger grains are known as gravel.

Sand Art

Dry grains of sand will flow through your fingers like water. Have you ever watched sand flow gently downward through a sand timer? Sand will not dissolve in water. When it becomes wet, it can be shaped and molded. Building sandcastles at the beach is a popular vacation pastime for grown-ups and children alike.

Sand Molds

Because wet sand holds its shape, you can use it to make molds (or casts). Choose simple shapes, such as the large shells and starfish shown here. Press them into a tray of damp sand to make the mold. Mix up some plaster, following the instructions on the packet. Carefully pour the plaster into the sand mold using a spoon. Leave the plaster to set hard. Then remove the shape, brushing away any loose sand with a stiff brush.

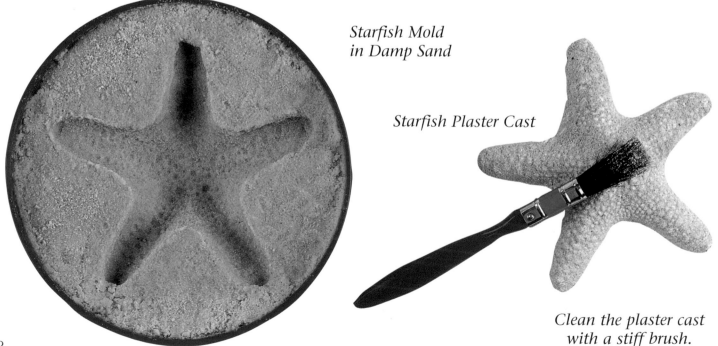

Starfish Mold in Damp Sand

Starfish Plaster Cast

Clean the plaster cast with a stiff brush.

Ripple Patterns in a Tray of Damp Sand

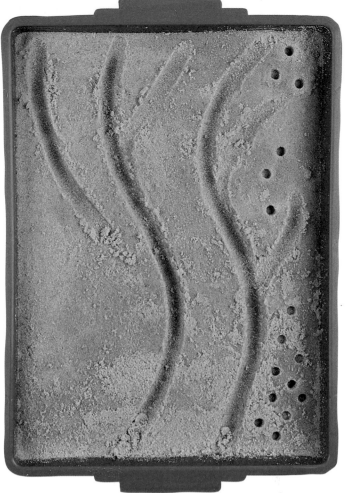

Patterns in Sand

As the sea washes over a sandy shore, moving in and out twice a day with the tides, rippled patterns are left behind in the wet sand. Raking patterns in sand around rocks is an art form found in traditional Japanese gardens. Such works of art are temporary by nature, because the wind and the rain will eventually make them disappear.

You can make patterns in damp sand and cast them in plaster to make a more permanent piece of sand art. Fill a tray or large bowl with damp sand. Use your fingers or wooden sticks to make abstract patterns in the sand. When you are happy with the design, carefully fill it with plaster, as explained opposite, and wait for it to set. Remove the hardened cast from the tray, brush away any loose sand, and paint the cast with poster paints.

Painted Plaster Casts

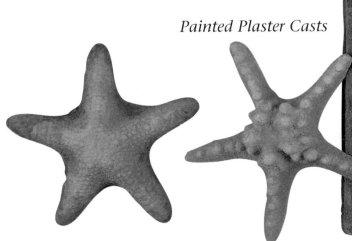

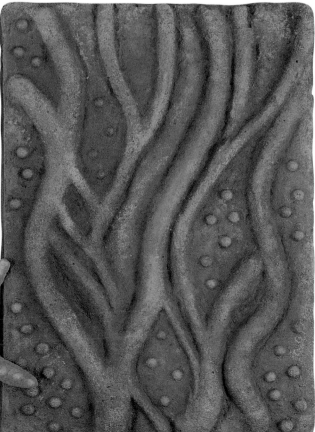

9

Rock Art

Words in Stone

Some of the oldest writing in the world has been preserved, because it is carved in stone. Egyptian stelae, which are carved columns of stone, can tell us much about Ancient Egypt. The Rosetta stone was found in 1799, and its Egyptian hieroglyphics (picture symbols) were figured out in 1822. Today, Mayan stelae are broken into small sections by robbers who want to sell them to collectors.

Icelanders scratched runes, another kind of picture writing, on stone. Pictures and symbols carved in stone are called *petroglyphs*. Neolithic hunters tattooed more than 100,000 such markings in the rocks of Parc de Mercantour in the South of France.

A Rock Collection

Paint soft, chalky rocks and make scratch marks in the surface with wooden tools.

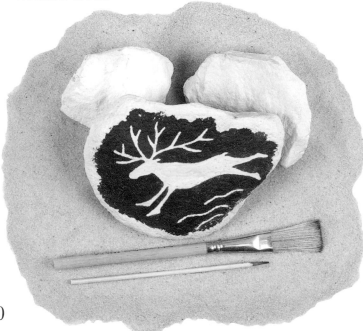

Rock Carvings

Early people often carved on nearby rocks, though carvings on soft rock have been worn-away over time. Fine examples of Bronze Age rock carvings of wild animals, ships, and sleds can be seen at Tanum, in Norway. Unfortunately, tourists and acid rain are wearing away these ancient works of art.

Collect as many different types of rock as you can find. Try making marks on the surfaces with different tools. Which rocks are easiest to carve?

*Stuffed
Paper Shape*

Rock Paintings

Some of the earliest rock paintings showing human and animal figures have been found in sandstone caves in Queensland, Australia. They are 25,000 years old. The red, yellow, and white tints have been made from iron oxides and kaolin pigments (colors).

In the middle of the Sahara desert, on the rocks of the Tassili Plateau, are paintings dating from 5000 B.C. At that time, the desert did not exist. Hunting scenes have been painted using pigments ground from the surrounding rocks. Powdered red, yellow, olive, and brown ochers and white kaolin were mixed with water, milk, or acacia gum.

Making a Rock Painting

Here is a way of making a painting that will look thousands of years old. Find some large sheets of strong paper, or glue sheets of newspaper together to make stronger sheets. Staple two pieces together around the edge, forming a large paper bag. Stuff the bag with crumpled scrap paper, securing the opening with staples. Paint the surface with a mixture of glue and sand. When dry this will give you a textured "rock" surface to paint. Look at examples of traditional rock paintings in books, then try painting your own.

*Rock
Painting*

Mud Prints

Grains of Silt

Like sand, silt or mud is also eroded grains of rock. But silt grains are smaller than sand grains. Silt grains are between 0.00015 in (0.004 mm) and 0.002 in (0.06 mm) across. Silt is carried by river water. When a river floods, this load of silt is deposited across the valley floor. The land of a flood plain is extremely fertile.

Muddy Shores

Where a large river carrying fresh water enters the sea, an estuary is formed. This is known as the mouth of the river. The water is filled with sediment, or silt. Often strong tides and currents carry the silt out to sea or along the shore. If the weight of the silt is heavy enough, it is deposited in the estuary and a delta is formed, like the Mississippi delta.

African Mud Cloths

In parts of Western Africa, mud is used to create patterns on cloth. The Korhogo of the Ivory Coast and the Bamana of Mali both decorate cloth using a mixture of mud and pigments. Their designs are painted on handwoven cotton cloth. The mud they use must be specially prepared. It stands, covered with water, in a clay pot for many months.

Making Mud Paints

If you live near a river estuary, it is the best place to collect mud. However, garden mud will do. Collect enough to fill a large container and mix with water. Filter the mud through a fine mesh strainer to remove any debris. When the mud is "clean," add some glue to make the paint. Try collecting mud from different places, to make a variety of colors. These can be stored in small containers until you need them.

Mud paints can be stored in jars.

Glue

Add glue to the clean mud and mix thoroughly to make the paint.

Making Mud Paints

Painting on Cloth

You can use mud pigments to paint on cloth. Use a piece of cotton cloth, from an old sheet, and cut it into a 12 sq in (30 sq cm) piece. Sketch your designs first on paper. African artists use simple, bold shapes on their textiles, like the ideas shown here.

Pin the cloth square to a large piece of thick cardboard to hold it taut while you work. Then trace your design on the cloth. Use the mud pigments to paint in the detail. You may need to add a small amount of water to the mud to make it easier to use.

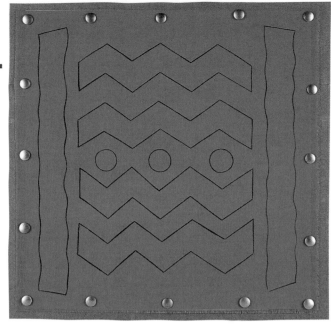

Cloth Stretched on Cardboard

Cloth with Frayed Edge

Shoulder Bag

Ideas for Mud Cloths

You may decide to make several painted square cloths. Give them a decorative frayed edge by pulling out the loose threads. Sew two square cloths together to make a cushion cover, or make them into an attractive shoulder bag by adding a shoulder strap.

13

Making A Mark

Clay Soil

Soil is weathered rock. Weathering happens in a number of ways. Extremes of temperature cause rocks to expand or contract, which then causes the rocks to crack. Water held in cracks may freeze, causing further cracking. Running water can dissolve or erode rock. Plants may grow in cracks, causing erosion. Dead plants help make fertile soil. Clay soil is eroded granite. All clays contain water.

Objects Useful for Making Impressions

Properties of Clay

Clay can be shaped. Primary clays are pure white and are used to make bone china. Secondary clays vary in color according to the minerals they contain. Pottery is fired clay. It has been heated in a kiln.

Clay Artifacts

Since early times, clay has been used to make pots. The first bricks were straw mixed with clay. They were used as a building material by the Romans. The domed roof of the Pantheon, built in Rome in A.D. 120, is made from bricks and concrete. Concrete is a mixture of cement (made from limestone and clay), sand, gravel, and water. Today, bricks are made from a mix of clay and sand.

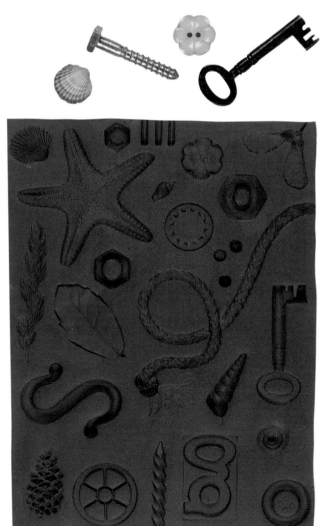

Clay Tile Impressed with the Objects Above

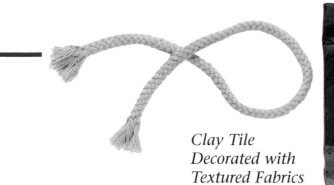

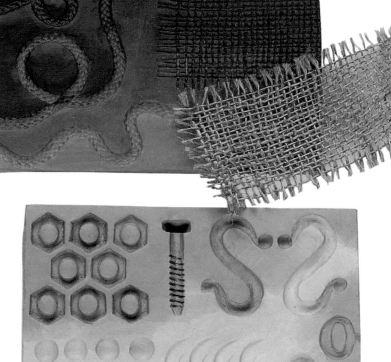

Clay Tile Decorated with Textured Fabrics

Impressions in Clay

A traditional method of decoration is to beat the clay with a cloth-covered paddle, leaving the imprint of the weave. In Northwest Cameroon, small carved wooden cylinders are rolled into strips of clay, leaving impressions. The strips are then built into the design of a pot.

Tools to make Impressions

Designs can be made in soft clay using a variety of everyday objects. You can use a self-hardening clay that does not need firing. Roll out the clay and make a series of tiles to practice on.

Collect different plastic and metallic objects, and use them to make interesting patterns in the clay. Try making impressions using fabrics with texture and natural materials, such as shells, seeds, fossils, and pieces of wood. Dust the objects with talcum powder first, to prevent them from sticking to the clay.

When you have made a series of patterned tiles, either use them to make plaster casts (see page 12) or leave them to harden. They can then be painted.

Clay Tile Decorated with Metal Objects

Clay Tile Decorated with Natural Materials

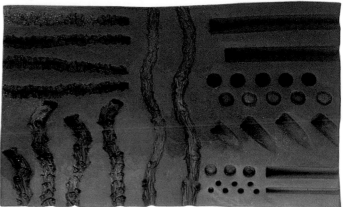

Clay Tile Decorated with Pieces of Wood 15

Raised Patterns

Gypsum

Gypsum was formed millions of years ago, when dinosaurs roamed the Earth. It is a white rock in which, for each molecule of gypsum, there are two molecules of water. It is mined all over the world. Gypsum is turned into plaster by crushing it into a powder. The water is removed by heating.

Alabaster

The Ancient Egyptians and the Romans created beautiful alabaster figures from a special kind of gypsum. The Ancient Egyptians coated the inside walls of their houses with white gypsum or plaster. They then painted the walls with colored patterns and scenes from nature. Noble Egyptian families had very elaborate wall paintings in their houses. The inside walls of the pyramids were also plastered, and decorated with pictures.

Plaster of Paris

Because gypsum was found in the Montmartre district of Paris, it became known as plaster of Paris. When plaster powder is mixed with water, it makes heat before hardening. This is because a chemical reaction takes place.

Natural Plaster Collage

Making Plaster Collages

A simple way of making a permanent natural collage is to collect grasses, leaves, and natural materials. Arrange and stick them on a thin piece of wood. Mix up a thin solution of plaster following the instructions on the packet, and brush it evenly over the collage. The plant forms will be preserved in the solid plaster.

16

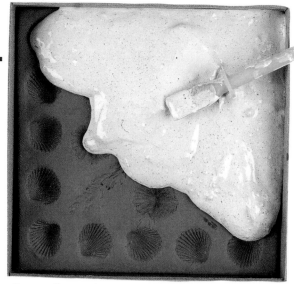

Spreading Plaster over the Mold

Care When Using Plaster

Cover all surfaces with newspaper before you begin. Mix the plaster in old plastic containers, these are easy to clean. Make sure the plaster mixture is free of lumps and bubbles. Work quickly. Never pour unused plaster down a drain.

Making Plaster Casts

There are examples of impressions in clay on the previous pages. While the clay remains soft, you can use impressed tiles as molds to make plaster reliefs. Place your patterned clay tile on to a flat board. Use pieces of thick card 2⅓ in (6 centimeters) wide to make a box structure around the tile, as shown here.

Mix up some plaster, following the instructions on the package. Pour a layer of about 2⅓ in (3 centimeters) evenly on top of the tile and leave to set. Then tear the cardboard sides off, and carefully remove the clay mold. Seal the plaster with watered-down glue before painting.

Plaster casts can be painted and varnished

Plaster Cast of Manufactured Objects

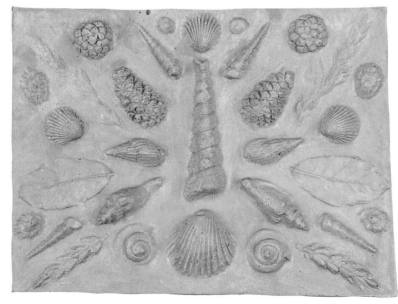

Plaster Cast of Natural Materials

Modeling with Clay

Pottery

Pottery-making is an ancient craft, carried out all over the world. Earth and water are combined by heat to create beautiful and useful artifacts. Archaeologists dig up fragments of pottery from which they can learn much about the past. In museums today, we can see fine examples of Ancient Greek pottery decorated with images of daily life and myths.

The shape and size of pots varies; they are usually made for a particular purpose. The earliest clay pots were shaped from coils of clay; thrown pots made on a wheel came later. Clay, containing traces of iron, turns a nice shade of red, known as *terra-cotta,* when the clay is fired. The words *terra* and *cotta* mean "baked earth."

Flatten the Base   *Hollow Out the Inside*

Making "Pebble" Pots

Here is an easy way to shape a clay pot with a lid. Mold a lump of clay in your hands, until it looks like a large, smooth pebble. Ask an adult to flatten one side to be the base, then carefully cut the "pebble" in half with a knife. The top half will be the lid, and the bottom will be the pot. Hollow the pieces, leaving the sides about ½ in (1 centimeter) thick.

Make textured patterns on the surfaces, or smooth out any unwanted marks with a damp sponge. Check that the lid still fits the pot. Leave to harden completely before painting with powder paints mixed with varnish.

Pebble Pots

Clay Whistles

The clay whistle is a traditional Central American wind instrument. Some have one mouthpiece opening, making only one note possible. An instrument from Chile called the ocarina has finger holes for playing scales.

Making a Bird Whistle

Take a lump of clay and mold it into a bird shape. Then cut the shape in half. Hollow out the two pieces and stick them together using a clay and water solution. Use a piece of ½ in (1 centimeter) wide dowel to make the blow-hole in the tail. Keep the dowel in place while the clay hardens, turning it gently to prevent it sticking. Make three small note holes on one side of the body.

When the clay is hard, cut out the whistle hole. Cut a 1½ in (4 cm) piece from the dowel to plug the blow-hole. The whistle noise is made by shaving the plug slightly, so air can blow through. You will need to adjust the plug and position it correctly in the blow-hole. Use non-toxic paint and varnish to decorate the whistle.

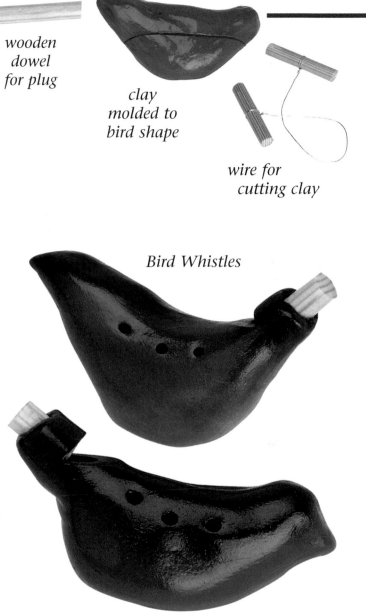

wooden dowel for plug

clay molded to bird shape

wire for cutting clay

Bird Whistles

Working with Self-Hardening Clay

You can use self-hardening clay to make these projects. The clay is easy to obtain in small quantities and does not need to be fired in a kiln. It contains a hardener and will set in a few days. When working on a project, keep the clay moist between sessions by wrapping the model in plastic wrap or a damp rag. Pieces of scrap wood, wire, plastic, and old kitchen utensils make ideal tools for clay modeling.

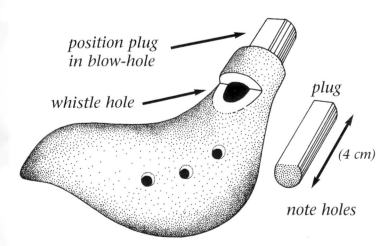

position plug in blow-hole

whistle hole

plug

(4 cm)

note holes

19

Plaster Carving

Symbolic Carvings

From the time that the first tools were made, craftspeople have felt the need to carve beautiful shapes. Wood, stone, plaster, and jade all lend themselves to this creative technique. Often such carvings were symbolic or religious. The elephant-headed Indian god, Ganesh, is often seen in sandalwood carvings. Vietnamese woodcarvers make figures that represent happiness or wealth to give as special gifts.

Tools and Materials

The color and character of the finished carving reflects the choice of material. The tools used will also be determined by the nature of the material. Wood can be cut, chiseled, or chopped, according to its type. Stone can be flaked, chipped, or pecked, depending upon its properties. Jade is difficult to carve because of its hardness.

Making a Plaster Block in a Cardboard Mold

Plaster Carving

Plaster is an ideal material to experiment with. It is inexpensive and easy to find. Being soft, it is easy to carve and shape with a few basic tools. Sketch your ideas first, drawing simple, solid shapes. You will be working in three dimensions, so think about the size and scale of your carving.

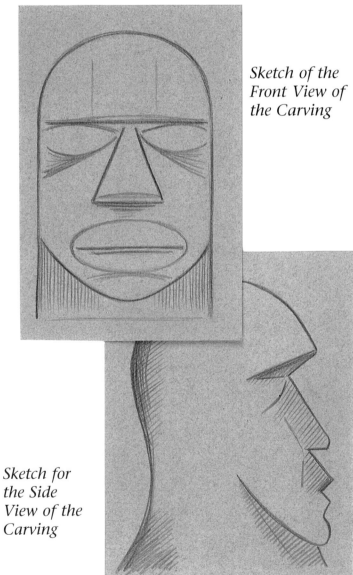

Sketch of the Front View of the Carving

Sketch for the Side View of the Carving

Carving Tools

*Carving Sketched
on a Plaster Block*

Making a Plaster Block

Make a cardboard mold large enough to cast the plaster block. You may even find a suitable plastic container to use. Mix up plaster following the instructions on the package. Pour it carefully into the mold and let it set. Tear off the cardboard, and let the block harden completely before starting to carve.

Preparing to Carve

Use your sketches and draw the shape of your carving on each side of the plaster block. This will be a rough guide when you begin to carve. Place your sketches in front of you, and keep checking them as you work.

Using Tools

An adult should always help you to use carpentry tools or kitchen utensils. Take care when carving large areas of plaster with a rasp, or chisel. As the carving takes shape, use smaller tools to cut out details, and smooth the surface with sandpaper. Seal the plaster with craft glue before painting and varnishing.

*Finished
Carvings*

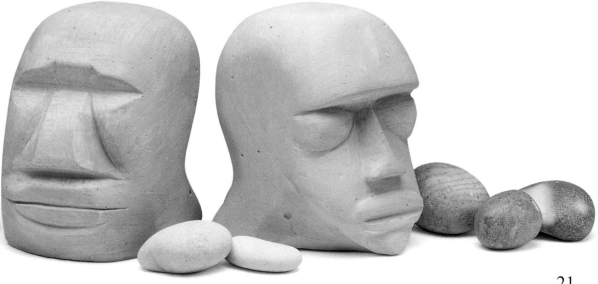

Natural Dyes

Symbolism and Color

Color in clothing has always been important, showing age, social position, and power. The use of color has different meanings in different countries. In the U.S. and Europe, black means sadness, but in China, white is the color of morning.

Natural Dyes

Minerals and plants were once the main sources of natural dyes. More unusual examples came from insects and mollusks. Purple was made from a rare Mediterranean species of whelk — it became a symbol of high position in the city of Rome. Insects like the South American cochineal beetle produce a range of red colors.

Vegetable Dyes Found in the Kitchen

Vegetable Dyes Found in the yard

Vegetable Dyes

Dyes can be obtained from roots, bark, berries, grasses, and leaves. Traditionally, plants that gave strong colors were highly regarded. Indigo and woad for blue, and madder for red are among the oldest plant dyes known. A bright golden yellow comes from the saffron crocus.

Experimenting with Vegetable Dyes

You can experiment with dyeing using common plant materials found in the kitchen and yard. Flowers, leaves, and berries should be collected fresh. Tougher materials like bark, fir cones, and walnut shells need to be chopped up and soaked in water overnight. Marigold and dahlia petals give yellows and browns, onion skins dye orange. Try tea, coffee, turmeric, or carrot tops.

Dyeing Equipment

Basic Equipment

For these experiments, gather together as many different dye stuffs as possible. Ask an adult to chop them up and boil them in water. Try dyeing scraps of white yarn or pieces of fleece, and find out how many shades of color you can create. A nail or piece of copper wire added to the dye bath (by an adult) will make the colors darker. Be sure to handle the nails or copper wire carefully. Wearing work gloves is a good idea.

Recording Experiments

It is important to keep a record of all your dyeing experiments. While you are working, make notes of when and where you collect the dye stuffs and how you prepared them. Make a loose-leaf record book and write up your results. Sketch or photograph the different plants and include samples of the dyed materials.

Dyeing Record Book

Onion Skins

1. Brown skins soaked overnight. Boiled & strained. Wool added to liquid and simmered for ½ hour

2. Copper wire added to dyebath.

3. Turmeric Powder

1 oz (25 gm). turmeric added to water and heated gently.

4. Wool added & simmered for ¼ hour.

4. Copper wire added.

Marigold petals — boiled in water.
Wool added and simmered for ½ hour.

Earth's Colors

Pigments and Paints

A pigment is used to give things color. Paint is made from a solid pigment mixed with a fluid. Dues dissolve in water, but pigments do not.

Paint is a colored substance that can be applied to a surface. The tools used to apply paint will vary with the nature of the paint. Oil paints are made by mixing pigments with linseed oil. Watercolors are a mixture of pigment and a water-soluble binder.

Color Wheel (below) Made From the Natural Materials (shown above right)

The Earliest Pigments

Clays, rocks, and metal ores provided the first pigments. In order to use them for painting, they were mixed with animal fats, gum arabic, beeswax, gelatine, or egg whites. The mineral lapiz lazuli gave ultramarine blue. The Egyptians crushed minerals like azurite, malachite, and cinnabar to obtain, respectively, blue, green, and vermilion red.

Natural Color Wheel

All the colors of the spectrum occur in nature. Climate and the changing seasons both have an effect on the color of plants. Make a collection of bright-colored natural materials, like feathers, minerals, shells, flowers, fruits, and vegetables, and arrange them into a natural color wheel.

Making Natural Colors

Medieval artists extracted pigments from flowers, berries, and leaves. A bright blue ink was made by crushing cornflower petals and mixing them with water. Oak galls were ground into paste and diluted to make black ink.

Experiment with the plants and fruits in your collection and make some watercolor paints. Flower petals, leaves, and berries can be mixed with a small amount of warm water. Squeeze the mixture through a strainer and use the colored juice like paint.

Earth Painting

Blow drops of paint with a drinking straw to make this tree landscape.

Natural Paints

Earth Painting

Watercolors made from flowers and berries are fun to experiment with, but the colors are very pale and quickly fade. Colors made from earth pigments are also easy to make and are much more permanent, as shown by cave paintings that have survived for many years.

Earth with lots of clay in it makes the best paint. Collect samples of different colored earths, also try using chalk and sand to get a range of colors. First sift any lumps and grit, then mix the earth with craft glue. The glue acts as a binder and makes the earth into a paint. The paints can be applied thickly or thinned out with water. Use them to paint an earth painting.

Earth Paints

Using Fibers

Sisal

Sisal is a fibrous plant that grew originally only in Central and South America. In the nineteenth century, it was introduced to East Africa, where the leaves were used to obtain a strong fiber. In Kenya, it is twined into kiondo bags, which are traditional round baskets. In Swaziland, it is used to make colorful coiled baskets.

Jute

The jute plant grows up to 157 in (4 metres) tall. The fibers are taken from the stem by soaking in water. They are much softer fibers than those obtained from sisal. About 70 percent of the world's jute is grown in Bangladesh. It was used to provide the raw material for rope, hessian, carpet backing, and sacking, but since the 1950s, artificial fibers have gradually been introduced.

Different Strings and Ropes Made From Natural Fibers

Hemp and Flax

It has been suggested that farmland could be planted with fiber crops for use in industry. Machines are being developed that can extract tough stem fibers from such plants on an industrial scale. Machines have already extracted fibers from hemp, flax, and even stinging nettles. Clothing can be woven from these fibers.

During the First World War (1914–1918), the Germans used nettle fibers to make a fabric similar to cotton. Even the waste from the process can be put to use. These woody granules, known as *shiv*, can be turned into animal bedding. Most importantly, hemp and flax fibers form a pulp from which paper can be made. They can also be added to recycled paper to restore its strength.

Useful Objects Made From Natural Fibers

Using Fibers

Different fibers are used to make rope and string for different purposes. Around the house and yard, rope and string have many uses. Coarse, strong rope is useful outdoors; fine string will tie up a package. See how many thicknesses and types of string you can find.

Coiling the String around a Plastic Container

Making String Bowls

Use scraps of string and rope from your collection to make a string bowl. Find a plastic container or plant pot to use as a mold. Brush craft glue on the outside, starting at the base and covering to a depth of 2 in (5 cm). Begin winding pieces of string around the container.

Continue glueing and winding the string, working around the outside of the container until it is completely covered. It may help to hold the string temporarily in place with masking tape. This can be removed when the glue dries and the wound string is firmly glued in place. Paint and varnish the finished bowls and use them as plant pots.

Coiled String Bowls

Straw Work

Harvest Time

All over the world, some people once believed that gods and goddesses were responsible for the harvest each year. In India, the corn spirit was Indra, the thunder god. He was thought to be responsible for the rice harvest. In Egypt, the story of Osiris was told. The Romans worshipped Ceres, the goddess of the harvest, from which the word *cereal* has come.

Harvest Emblems

In India today, designs in straw are made with rice straw. They are hung in doorways as good luck charms when young couples marry. The designs are usually in the shape of everyday objects like combs. Sometimes a ram's horn shape is made.

In the United States, corn dolls were once harvest emblems made as offerings of thanks to the gods, or idols, for the crops. It is from "idol" that the word dolly comes. Native Americans once used corn husks for weaving cloth or wrapping food. When corn husks have been softened in glycerine and water, they can also be used to shape doll figures.

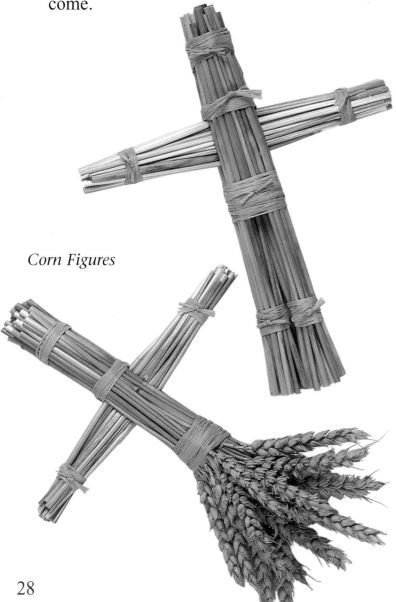

Corn Figures

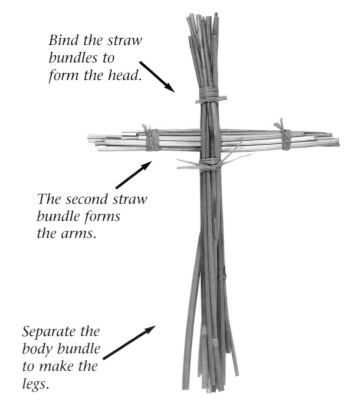

Bind the straw bundles to form the head.

The second straw bundle forms the arms.

Separate the body bundle to make the legs.

Making Corn Figures

By binding pieces of straw together with raffia, you can make a family of corn figures. Start by making small bundles, trimming the straw and tying it with raffia or thread. Make up the figures as shown here. A larger bundle forms the body, with a thinner piece shaping the arms. Try making animal figures in the same way.

Making a Scarecrow

The scarecrow is made in a similar way to the corn figures, but on a larger scale. You will need a bunch of straw, or thin twigs and branches could also be used, if available. A large bundle of straw forms the main body structure, with smaller, thinner shapes for the arms and legs.

Bind the body together with raffia or string. You can then dress the scarecrow in old clothes, and stand it in the vegetable garden.

Natural Materials

Scarecrow

Glossary

alabaster A variety of gypsum which is usually white in color.

cobble stones Large, naturally rounded stones found on certain seashores. Not the same as the cobble stones used in road building.

dyes Substances used to stain or color.

elements Substances that make up the universe. Scientists know of more than 105 elements, each of which contains only one kind of atom.

estuary The part of a river mouth where sea and river water meet and mix.

fibers Natural or synthetic filaments that can be spun into yarn.

germs Tiny living things that are hard using just your eyes and they can cause you harm.

gypsum A mineral of hydrated calcium sulphate found in sedimentary rocks. Used to make plaster.

hieroglyphics An ancient form of writing used in Ancient Egypt in which pictures or symbols represent objects, ideas, and sounds.

iron oxides Seen as rust on the surface of iron, where the iron has reacted with water and oxygen.

kaolin A fine white clay used to make bone china and porcelain — also known as china clay.

lava Hot magma that flows from an erupting volcano. Igneous rock is solidified lava.

molecule A molecule is the simplest unit of a chemical compound and is formed when two or more atoms combine chemically.

mollusk An invertebrate with a soft, unsegmented body and often a shell. Gastropods, cephalopods, and bivalves are all mollusks.

ochers Various natural earths containing ferric oxide, silica, and alumina used as yellow and red pigments.

petroglyphs Pictures and inscriptions carved in stone.

pigments Substances found in plant or animal tissue that produce a characteristic color.

plaster of Paris A white powder that sets hard when mixed with water because a chemical reaction occurs. It is so-called because it was found in the Montmartre district of Paris.

raffia A fiber obtained from the stalks of certain palm trees and used for weaving.

runes Writing symbols from an ancient Germanic alphabet used in Scandinavia, up to and during the Middle Ages.

terra-cotta Unglazed clay or earthenware pottery that is reddish-brown in color.

For More Information

Books to Read

Imagine Your World in Clay, Maureen Carlson (North Light Books, 2005)

Let's Rock (Painting on Rocks for Kids), Linda Kranz (Northwood Press, 2003)

Native American Rock Art (Messages from the Past), Yvette Lapierre (Charlesbridge Publishing, 1994)

Nature Crafts, Joy Williams (North Light Books, 2002)

Nature's Art Box, Laura C Martin (Storey Publishing, 2003)

The Kids Multi-Cultural Craft Book, Roberta Gould (Williamson Publishing Company, 2003)

The Super Duper Art and Craft Activity Book, Lynn Gordon (Chronicle Books, 2005)

Places to visit

American Visionary Art Museum,
800 Key Highway, Baltimore, Maryland 21230
(Displaying art from recycled materials including customised 'Art Cars', sculpture, and mosaics)

Boston Children's Museum,
300 Congress Street, Boston MA 02210
(Includes The Recycle Shop, a children's activity center where re-used materials can be transformed into art projects, and weaving exhibits, including large-scale looms for children to use.)

Frisco Native American Museum and Natural History Center, Hwy 12, Frisco, NC
(Native American artefacts, art, and culture)

Metropolitan Museum of Art,
1000 Fifth Avenue, New York, New York 10028
(Wide range of exhibits, including jewelry, mosaics, sculpture, block printing, and textiles and dyeing)

UCM Museum, 22275 Hwy 36,
Abita Springs, LA 70420, Ph: 985-892-2624
(Small, eccentric collection of art made from recycled materials, mosaics, and more)

Web Sites

Due to the changing nature of Internet links, PowerKids Press has developed an online list of Web sites related to the subject of this book. This site is regularly updated. Please use this link to access this list: www.powerkidslinks.com/everydayart/sandandearth

Index